The Railway Revolution

Written by Jo Nelson

Contents

Collins

The power of the railways

The railways changed everything in Britain: where people lived, worked and went on holiday, where they shopped and what they ate. Linking the towns and cities with a network of fast transport routes brought people closer together and helped businesses to grow. It even made professional football possible, by giving teams and their fans a way to travel around the country for matches.

Arsenal fans catching a special train to see their team play.

Before trains

It's hard to imagine a world without high-speed travel, but around 200 years ago life was very different. There were no railways or trains, no motorways or cars and definitely no planes. Most people didn't even try to travel long distances. Those who needed to make a journey would either go on foot, by horse, or in a horse-drawn carriage known as a stagecoach.

Stagecoaches

Stagecoaches got their name because they travelled in stages, stopping every 16 to 24 kilometres to rest the horses. Journeys by stagecoach were slow and uncomfortable, and breakdowns were frequent.

There wasn't a network of well-maintained roads, just a series of rough, pot-holed tracks. The tracks became thick with mud when it rained, bumpy with ridges when the mud dried and impossible to use in the snow.

A journey of 645 kilometres from London to Edinburgh would typically take two weeks by stagecoach. Today it takes around seven hours by car or five hours by train.

two stagecoaches passing on a dusty track

Rivers

Transporting heavy goods was even harder than taking passengers. There was a limit on how much weight a couple of horses could pull in a wagon, or a horse or donkey could take on its back. Where possible, goods were transported by boat, but there simply weren't enough large rivers for boats to get around Britain! That's why people started digging canals.

In the 1700s, the River Irwell was made into a useful trade route into Manchester.

a donkey carrying goods

5

Canals

The canals were narrow, shallow channels of water with narrow, shallow boats to match, known as narrowboats. Engines weren't used successfully to power vehicles until the 19th century so it was up to horses again to pull the boats along.

The boats' **cargo** ranged from stone and coal to cotton, grain and **manufactured** goods. Most of the cargo's weight was supported by the water, but journeys by canal could take weeks, even months.

At best, the boats could only travel at walking speed! Then there was the extra time needed to operate the complicated canal locks, the rest time needed to save the horses from exhaustion and the days when no boats could move because the canals were frozen solid.

However, until a better idea came along, canals were still an extremely useful way to shift large deliveries – and the demand for transporting heavy loads was getting greater by the day.

Canal locks took water and boats up and down changes in ground level through a clever system of gates.

Changing Britain

Britain was changing from being a land of farms and small villages to a land of factories and big cities. The first factories were mills by rivers, which used water power to operate heavy machinery. From around 1780, steam engines were being used in factories as well.

Machines could make products more quickly and cheaply than people simply working by hand. Cheaper products meant more people could afford them and the demand increased. Soon hundreds of factories were opening across Britain, creating jobs in towns and cities and encouraging people to move from the countryside.

More canals were dug out to supply factories with **raw materials** and take away finished products. It could take the narrowboats weeks to deliver their loads, but people just had to wait.

Water power was used to operate millstones, which crushed grain into flour.

Inventing the steam train

It seems obvious now that trains on rail tracks would be much faster and more **efficient** than narrowboats on canals, but it took some hard-working inventors and some impressive technology to make that leap.

The idea of using rail tracks wasn't new. Miners already used tracks to pull their carts along, sometimes known as "waggonways". As far back as the 6th century BCE, the ancient Greeks carved tracks into stone for horses to drag carts along. But it was a long time before anyone came up with a better driving force than horsepower.

Horses working in mines were called pit ponies.

Early steam power

The idea of trying to use steam wasn't new either. Inventors had been interested in steam power for centuries, but the first truly successful steam engines didn't appear until the 18th century. Nicknamed "miners' friends", they were stationary engines – engines in fixed positions – that used steam pressure to pump water out of underground mines.

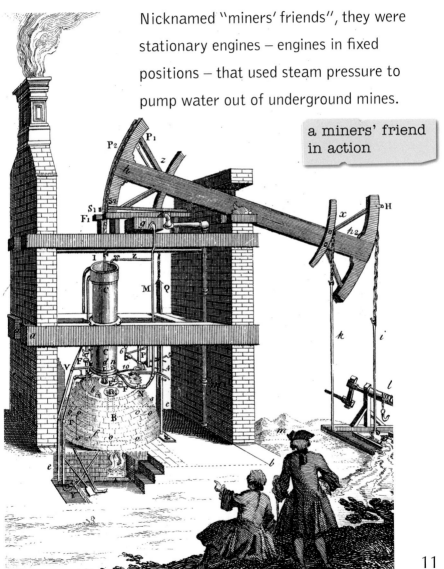

a miners' friend in action

Nicolas-Joseph Cugnot

In 1770, French inventor Nicolas-Joseph Cugnot used a steam engine to create the world's first self-propelled mechanical vehicle. It was, quite literally, a vehicle that could move under its own steam. However, it was heavy, unstable and very slow. It took a quarter of an hour to travel half a kilometre and blocked the way for everyone else!

Cugnot's vehicle was difficult to steer, and ran into a wall.

Richard Trevithick

Richard Trevithick, born in 1771, was the son of a Cornish mine manager. As a child he was fascinated by the "miners' friends" and would watch them pump water from deep underground. When he grew up, he became an **engineer** at one of the mines and began experimenting with different engine designs.

Trevithick found a way to use high-pressure steam in an engine to make it more powerful. He then set about using the engine to drive a vehicle. By 1801, he'd built his first full-sized steam vehicle – Puffing Devil. He drove it successfully, reaching a top speed of 17 kilometres per hour, but it could only manage short journeys.

Puffing Devil

side view   front view

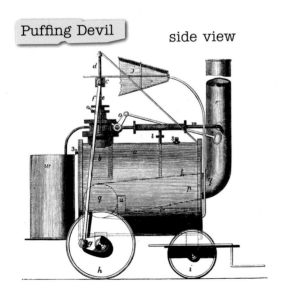
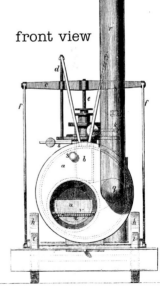

The first steam locomotive

Trevithick was asked to build a high-pressure, stationary steam engine to operate a hammer at an **ironworks** in Wales. The owner of the ironworks, Samuel Homfrey, was impressed with the engine – but he was even more impressed when Trevithick mounted it on wheels and showed how it could be used as a **locomotive** to pull heavy carts.

Homfrey made a bet with a friend that Trevithick's locomotive could pull ten tonnes of iron along a 16-kilometre stretch of rail track that led to the ironworks. Word spread about the bet and, on 21 February 1804, a crowd of spectators gathered to watch the attempt.

Sure enough, Trevithick's engine on wheels managed to pull the ten tonnes of iron – as well as five wagons and 70 men. It took four hours and five minutes, travelling at an average speed of 3.9 kilometres per hour.

Encouraged by this success, Trevithick built a new locomotive named Catch-me-who-can to show off to the public in Euston Square, London. People could pay one shilling for a ride around a circular track. Sadly, the rails weren't strong enough and the locomotive eventually toppled over.

After that, Trevithick gave up on steam locomotives. His idea was right, but it would take someone else to turn it into a success.

Trevithick's Catch-me-who-can locomotive on its circular track

George Stephenson

The inventor of the first useful steam train was
George Stephenson. His father worked as a fireman at
a coalmine in Northumberland, stoking the "miners' friends".
He couldn't afford to send his son to school. Instead, George
spent hours with his father, learning about engines.

Stephenson only learnt to read and write at the age of 18, when he was earning his own money and could pay for himself to go to evening classes. He'd work with engines in the mines by day and study engineering by night.

Stephenson had heard about engines pulling wagons along tracks and decided to design one for the coalmine where he worked. In 1814, he completed his first locomotive. It could travel uphill at 6.4 kilometres per hour.

Stephenson named his locomotive "Blücher".

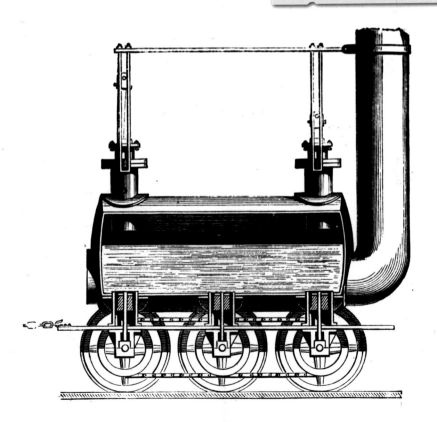

Between 1814 and 1821, Stephenson designed 17 different locomotives to use at coalmines. He included a special wheel shape, with an extra ridge on the inside to help keep the train on the track.

Improved steam locomotives were no good if the tracks they ran on kept breaking, so Stephenson also worked on improving rail track designs. Iron rails were much better than the earlier wooden ones, but it was important to spread the weight of the engine and carts to prevent the metal from cracking.

In 1820, Stephenson was hired to build a 13-kilometre stretch of rail track from Hetton coalmine in County Durham to the nearest river where boats could dock. It opened in 1822 and was the world's first railway to run without using animal power.

Stephenson's locomotives at Hetton coalmine

Stephenson's next major construction was the 40-kilometre Stockton and Darlington Railway, connecting coalmines to Darlington and to the River Tees at Stockton. By now, Stephenson had his son Robert working with him and together they set up a company to make steam locomotives for the line.

On 27 September 1825, the railway was officially opened to great fanfare. Stephenson himself was in the driving seat of his newly-built Locomotion engine, pulling the world's first passenger carriage, Experiment, plus 21 coal wagons fitted with seats and more wagons piled with coal and flour.

Over 450 passengers clambered aboard and thousands more turned out to watch the exciting event. At times, the train reached a top speed of 24 kilometres per hour and left men on horseback trailing far behind. The journey was reported in newspapers around the country. For the first time in human history, people were able to travel faster than a galloping horse!

the Stockton and Darlington Railway

The Liverpool and Manchester Railway

Across the country, merchants and factory owners were beginning to see the appeal of the railways and all eyes were now turned to see if the next major project – the Liverpool and Manchester Railway – would be a success.

In 1829, with the railway line nearing completion, its directors needed to decide how their wagons would be pulled. One option was to use stationary steam engines which would pull the trains on long cables, but the directors were keen to see if any locomotives were up to the task instead.

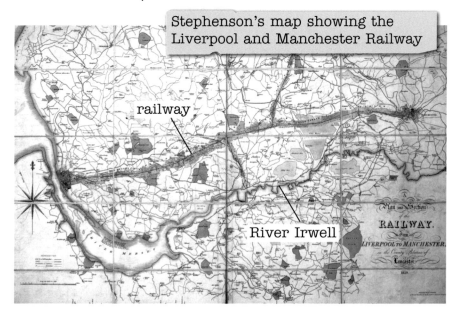

Stephenson's map showing the Liverpool and Manchester Railway

railway

River Irwell

They announced a competition to find the best locomotive and devised a series of trials on a stretch of the railway at Rainhill. The locomotives were required to pull a train of 20 tonnes at a speed of 16 kilometres per hour – and not just as a one-off. To prove they were up to the task, they had to complete ten return trips. The owners of the winning locomotive would then receive £500 in prize money (around £715,000 in today's money).

two of the competition entries

The Novelty
by Braithwaite
and Erricsson

The Sanspareil
by Hackworth

The Rainhill trials

The trials began on 6 October 1829. There were only five entries: four steam-powered locomotives, including Rocket designed by George and Robert Stephenson, and a horse-powered locomotive named Cycloped.

Cycloped was the first to drop out. Its power came from a horse walking on a treadmill and it was never going to achieve the required speed on the track.

As the horse walked on the treadmill, the wheels turned on the track.

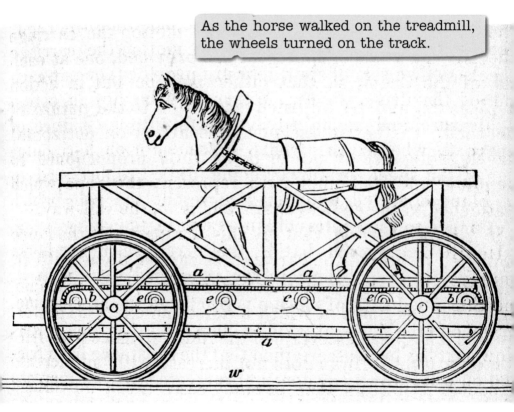

One by one, the other locomotives dropped out as things went wrong with their engines, until only Stephensons' Rocket was left. With George Stephenson as the driver once more, the Rocket was achieving an average speed of 22.5 kilometres per hour along the 2.4-kilometre track. Then, on the final trip, George really went for it – and averaged nearly 48 kilometres per hour!

That's twice the speed his Locomotion engine managed, only four years earlier.

The £500 prize money was won by the Stephensons. They were commissioned to make four more steam locomotives to operate on the new line.

the Stephensons' Rocket

25

Railway dangers

The Liverpool and Manchester Railway
officially opened on 15 September 1830.
It was the first railway to be operated solely by
steam locomotives.

Unfortunately, there was a dreadful accident at
the grand opening celebration. William Huskisson,
Member of **Parliament** for Liverpool, ignored
warnings to stay off the track and was run over
by one of the locomotives. His death added to
people's fears around the country over the safety
of the railways.

As well as the obvious danger of oncoming trains,
there were concerns that passengers' eyesight
could be damaged by the fast-moving scenery or
that sudden jolts would upset their stomachs.

Government ministers argued in parliament
that houses near the line would be set on fire
from engine sparks, that the boiler engines could
explode and blow up passengers, or that farm
animals would be disturbed along the routes and
that poisoned air might kill the birds.

the grand opening of the Liverpool and Manchester Railway

27

Rolling out the track

In the end, none of these fears could outweigh the huge benefits the railways offered. The age of the steam train had begun and people across Britain were keen to get on board.

The rapid expansion of the railway network over the next few decades was astonishing. By 1835, there were 483 kilometres of railway track in Britain. By 1840, there were 2,409 kilometres and by 1850, there were over 9,600 kilometres. The railway lines crisscrossed Britain, from Aberdeen in Scotland down to Plymouth in the south-west of England. It had taken only 20 years for a completely new transport system to be established.

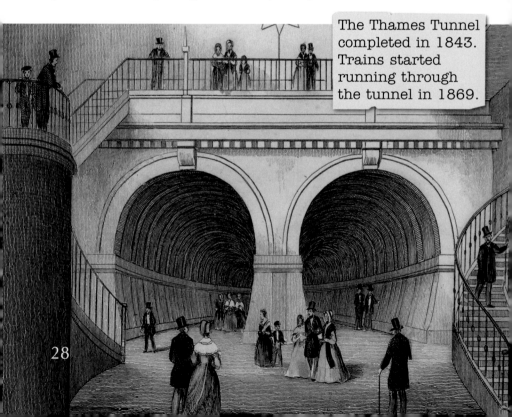

The Thames Tunnel completed in 1843. Trains started running through the tunnel in 1869.

Canals continued to play a significant role in delivering raw materials to factories, but anyone planning a new transport route now chose laying down a railway over digging out a canal.

New railway lines stretched across the country.

All aboard!

Although the railways had originally been invented to move heavy goods more easily, they were highly appealing to passengers too. Not only were journeys by train three times quicker than by stagecoach, they were also half the price.

It would be another 50 years before the motorcar was invented and improved roads could begin to compete with the railways. In the meantime, rail travel was fast transforming everyday life.

In order to attract the most customers, train operators introduced three different types of carriages, with three different ticket prices to match.

Third class

The cheapest seats were in third class, in open-topped carriages. Passengers sat packed together on wooden boards, exposed to the wind and rain, but they didn't mind. For many, this was their first opportunity to travel further than their feet would take them.

open-topped carriages packed with passengers

A trip to the seaside became a popular day out, and seaside businesses began to benefit from visitors spending money in their town.

Railway companies produced posters encouraging people to take a trip to the seaside.

Second class

Those with more money could choose to travel second class. Their carriages were just as crowded as third class, but at least they had a roof to keep out the worst of the weather.

Regular, affordable train services opened up new opportunities for where people might live. Instead of having a house within walking distance of their place of work, they could live near a train station and **commute** instead!

a second-class carriage

First class

At the top end of the scale were first-class carriages, with sides as well as a roof and padded seats. Wealthy people would pay a higher price for this respectable way to travel and make day trips into the city, perhaps for a shopping excursion or to see an exhibition.

THERE ARE 1ST CLASS COMPARTMENTS ON ALL TRAINS SERVING THIS STATION FOR THOSE HOLDING 1ST CLASS TICKETS

SOUTHERN RAILWAY

First-class carriages were much more comfortable!

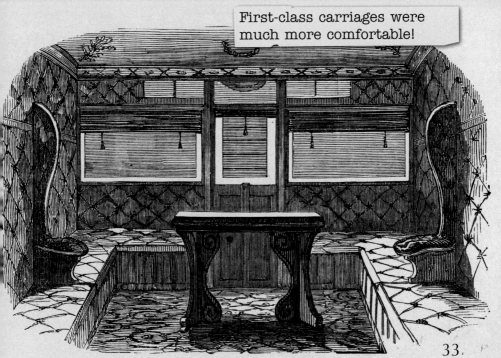

Railway planning

Laying down hundreds of kilometres of track took careful planning, innovative engineering and thousands of hard-working people.

Each new railway route had to be carefully considered and approved by parliament. Although there was often strong opposition from people living close to the proposed line, the railway companies usually won in the end.

The London and Birmingham Railway went straight through Camden Town, North London.

Rich landowners received large sums of money for allowing train lines to run through their land, but poorer, working-class people could be kicked out of their homes with very little **compensation**. In London alone, between 1853 and 1901, around 76,000 people had their homes demolished to make way for railways and train stations.

Once the basic route was approved, engineers would work out the best way to lay tracks across tricky sections of the line. Even a gradual uphill slope could reduce the power of a steam locomotive by half. However, laying down flat tracks wasn't always an option because hills, valleys, rivers and bogs all got in the way.

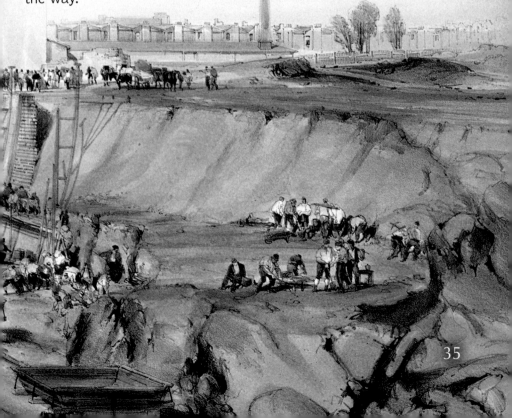

Railway engineering

Two of the great railway engineers of the 19th century were George Stephenson himself and Isambard Brunel. They looked to the canals for inspiration and here are some of the ideas they came up with.

cuttings – cutting out routes through raised sections of land

embankments – building up routes across low sections of land

viaducts – constructing long bridges to carry tracks across a valley

tunnels – digging underground routes through hills

Stephenson even managed to cross a tricky section of bog by floating the rails on a bed of heather and wood, covered with a layer of stone.

Brunel's great railway

Isambard Brunel, born in 1806, was the son of a French engineer. In his early twenties, he worked as an assistant on his father's project to build a tunnel under the River Thames in London. Then, in 1833, he became chief engineer on an ambitious railway project – the Great Western Railway, linking London to Bristol. Brunel's ground-breaking designs included the world's widest brick arch bridge and longest railway tunnel at that time.

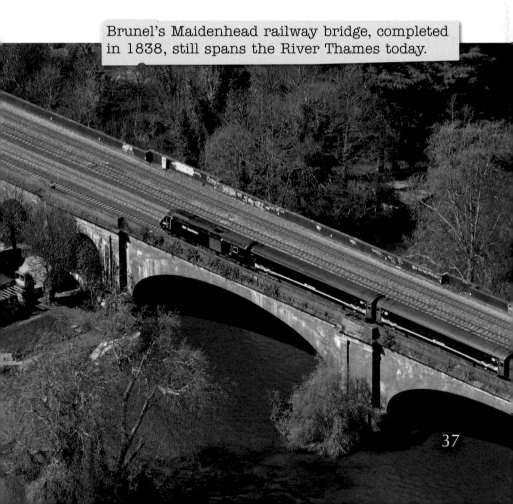

Brunel's Maidenhead railway bridge, completed in 1838, still spans the River Thames today.

Manpower

Designing railways was tricky, but actually constructing them was backbreaking, exhausting and downright dangerous. Each project required thousands of labourers, working only with simple hand tools such as picks, shovels and wheelbarrows.

In the 1850s, there were as many as 250,000 – a quarter of a million – labourers building new railways in Britain. They were nicknamed "navvies", because before the railways the main labouring job had been constructing **navigation** routes for boats, also known as canals!

Men and women came from all over the British Isles to work as navvies. They received higher pay than factory workers, but had to put up with basic, cramped living conditions, in temporary wooden huts.

Work accidents were common, particularly in the construction of tunnels, where gunpowder was used to blast through hillsides and rock falls were common. 26 people died in the construction of the first Woodhead tunnel in the north of England, completed in 1845. The deaths prompted a public enquiry and eventually led to new safety laws and compensation for injuries.

It was hard, dirty work being a navvy.

Railway jobs

Once a railway was complete, a large workforce was needed to keep the trains running. Many people dreamt of becoming an engine driver, but first they had to work their way through the ranks, starting as an engine cleaner, and then being promoted to fireman.

The engine cleaner had the unpleasant job of crawling into the steam engine firebox when it was cold, and shovelling out the leftover pieces of coal.

The fireman had the slightly better job of keeping the engine fed with coal throughout its journey. It was sooty, sweaty and physically demanding, but worth sticking at if you wanted to become an engine driver.

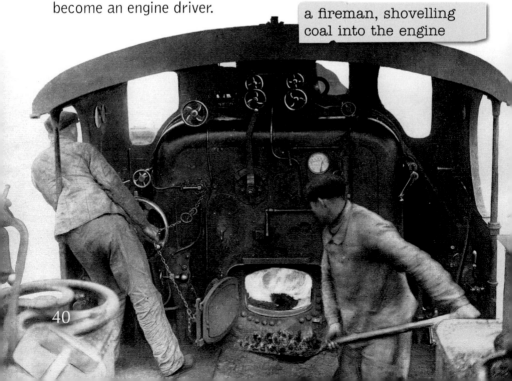

a fireman, shovelling coal into the engine

Signalmen worked from little signal boxes beside the railways, indicating to passing trains whether the line ahead was clear. They would write down the timings of each train and pass the information to the next signalman via a series of bell codes sent along telegraph wires.

There were jobs in the stations too. Each station would be run by a stationmaster and have a range of employees, including ticket officers and railway guards.

a railway guard

Transforming transport

By 1850, railways across Britain and the factories they served had made Britain the richest country in the world. People's lifestyles had been transformed by the railways – and not just through new travel opportunities.

Farmers and fishermen could now sell fresh meat, dairy, vegetables and fish to people living in cities.

National newspapers could now be delivered by train, keeping people up-to-date with what was happening across the country.

"Mail trains" could deliver letters and parcels more swiftly than ever before.

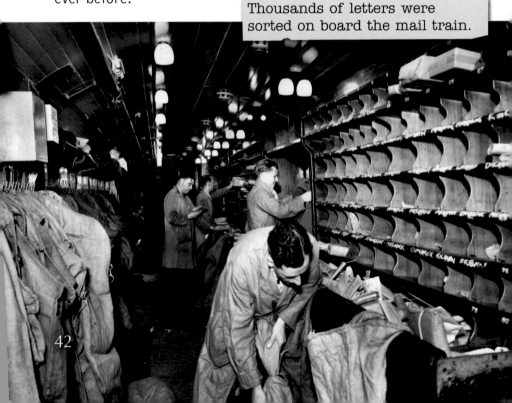

Thousands of letters were sorted on board the mail train.

In the event of a riot or protest, the government could quickly send soldiers to the trouble spot by train.

The railways even prompted the government to introduce the same time across the country, known as standard time, so everyone's clock said the same thing and the trains could run on time.

Imagine how different the world would've been if trains hadn't been invented when they were. If they'd arrived 50 years earlier, we'd have had hardly any canals; 50 years later and every city might have been linked by water! By the end of the 19th century, road travel began to take off. If trains hadn't arrived before cars, then they might never have been part of our transport system!

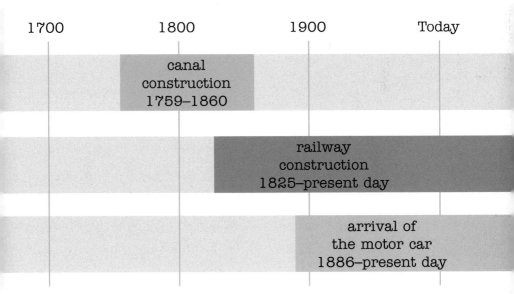

1700	1800	1900	Today

canal
construction
1759–1860

railway
construction
1825–present day

arrival of
the motor car
1886–present day

American railroads

Britain wasn't the only country investing heavily in railways. Around the same time that George Stephenson was building his first steam locomotives, Americans across the Atlantic were experimenting with model railways and testing English steam designs on their newly-constructed railway lines, known in America as railroads.

Before long, American engineers were designing their own steam locomotives and rolling out hundreds of kilometres of railroads across their vast country, to carry both passengers and freight, including cotton, granite, grain, cattle and coal.

In 1830, there were around 120 kilometres of railroad track in America. By 1840, there were 4,500 kilometres, by 1860 there were 46,679 kilometres and by 1890, there were around 264,000 kilometres!

In 1869, the first railroad to link the west of America with the east was completed. Named the First Transcontinental Railroad, it was an impressive achievement – not only because of the tricky **terrain** and sheer distance covered, but also because two railroad companies starting from opposite sides of the country had to meet at an exact point in the middle! The final track was 2,858 kilometres long and reduced the journey time across America from six months to a week.

The two main railroads in America, finally meeting in the middle!

Trains were quick to catch on in Europe, as well. Governments found that railways could boost their country's businesses by providing new jobs and creating new markets for local products. The railway lines also linked neighbouring countries and opened up a new era of international travel.

The Orient Express

In 1883, a **luxury** train service began taking passengers from Paris to Constantinople (now Istanbul). It was called the Orient Express and it included sleeping carriages, day carriages and a restaurant carriage, all beautifully furnished and decorated to rival the finest hotels in the world. Kings and presidents were among the passengers, as were numerous spies who found the train an easy way to pass between different countries.

a poster advertising the Orient Express

The Trans-Siberian Railway

The longest railway line in the world is the Trans-Siberian Railway, which stretches the width of Russia, from Moscow in the west to the port of Vladivostok in the east – a distance of 9,299 kilometres. It was built between 1891 and 1916 and is still being extended today.

Running out of steam

By the beginning of the 20th century, countries all over the world, from Cuba and Mexico to India and Pakistan, were crisscrossed by rail tracks. Motor vehicles and improved roads provided alternatives to rail travel, but they didn't replace it. Trains were here to stay – although not necessarily pulled by steam locomotives.

In towns and cities, efforts were being made to reduce the smoke and noise of steam trains by introducing electric trams. The trams got their power from electric wires suspended above the track, so they were much quieter and cleaner.

an electric tram running through Lisbon, Portugal

48

By 1920, railway tracks outside of towns were being **electrified** too, and a new type of locomotive that used a **diesel** engine to generate electricity was invented.

As diesel engine designs improved, diesel locomotives gradually took over from steam ones. They were cleaner, faster and more efficient. However, many people missed the hiss of the steam train and its familiar plume of smoke. To this day, some train lines still run steam trains for pleasure rides and special occasions.

Railways now have super-fast air travel to compete with as well as roads, but they continue to find new ways to attract passengers.

Undersea trains

In 1988, the Seikan Tunnel opened in Japan, taking a railway line deep beneath the seabed to link the main island of Japan with an island to the north. Six years later, another undersea tunnel – the Channel Tunnel – opened, linking England to France. Trains can now travel beneath the 37.8-kilometre stretch of sea at speeds of up to 159 kilometres per hour.

Engineers and workmen celebrate as the first part of the Channel Tunnel is finished.

High-speed rail

Many countries are now investing in designated high-speed train lines, to enable long-distance trains to go even faster. Japan led the way in the 1960s with their electric "bullet" trains between Tokyo and Osaka. Today, high-speed trains can travel at around 290 kilometres per hour, greatly improving intercity travel.

the bullet train passing Mount Fuji in Japan

Magnetic trains

The fastest trains to date use magnetic power and don't even touch the tracks! They're known as "maglev" trains, short for magnetic levitation.

Currently, maglev trains can reach speeds of around 435 kilometres per hour, but future designs are likely to whizz along at over 483 kilometres.

Watch this space – the railway revolution isn't over yet!

Glossary

BCE stands for Before the Common Era – the same as BC

cargo load carried by a vehicle

commute travel to and from work

compensation payment to cover loss

diesel a type of fuel

efficient without wasting time and effort

electrified made ready to run off electricity

engineer someone who works with engines

ironworks where iron is removed from rock, and iron objects are made

locomotive a self-propelled vehicle

luxury elegant, expensive and very comfortable

manufactured made by hand or by machinery

navigation movement in a planned direction

parliament group of people responsible for making a country's laws

raw materials the basic materials used to make things, e.g. wood or coal

terrain land surface

Index

Train timetable

1830
Liverpool and
Manchester Railway

1825
The Stockton and
Darlington Railway

1804
Catch-me-who-can

1770
mechanical vehicle

1771
Puffing Devil

1814
Blücher

1829
Rocket

18th century
miners' friends

1835
483 kilometres of
track in Britain

**The present
and future**
maglev train

1850
9,600 kilometres
of track in Britain

1916
Trans-Siberian Railway

1920
diesel engines

1883
Orient Express

1960
bullet train

1869
First Transcontinental
Railroad

Ideas for reading

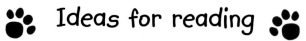

Written by Clare Dowdall, PhD
Lecturer and Primary Literacy Consultant

Reading objectives
- make comparisons within and across books
- summarise the main ideas drawn from more than one paragraph, identifying key details that support the main ideas
- retrieve, record and present information from non-fiction
- explain and discuss their understanding of what they have read, including through formal presentations and debates, maintaining a focus on the topic and using notes where necessary

Spoken language objectives:
- participate in discussions, presentations, performances, role play, improvisations and debates

Curriculum links: History – Victorian England

Resources: ICT, maps showing rail routes, paper and pencils.

Build a context for reading
- Read the title and blurb together and ask children to suggest what they think the title *The Railway Revolution* means.
- Discuss what the children know already about the development of rail travel. Ask them to compare the two trains shown on the front cover and describe how they are different.
- Ask children to share their experiences of travelling on different sorts of trains and train journeys.

Understand and apply reading strategies
- Read pp2–3 together, ask children to imagine what life was like 200 years ago without trains and cars. Discuss what they wouldn't have been able to do that they can do now.
- Model how to read and summarise key ideas about stagecoach travel (p4). Draw facts and present them concisely.
- Challenge children to follow this model to read and summarise the key ideas about river transport (pp5–7).